107 Marketing and Lead Generation Tips to Turbocharge Your Business in 60 Days or Less

By George J Wells

Copyright © 2018 by George J Wells

All rights reserved. No part of this publication may be reproduced, disturbed, or stored in any form by any means, including photocopying, recording, or other electronic or mechanical methods, without the prior written permission of the publisher, except in the case of brief quotations embodied in critical reviews and certain other noncommercial uses permitted by copyright law.

Disclaimer

Although the author and publisher have made every effort to ensure that the information in this book was correct at press time, the author and publisher do not assume and hereby disclaim any liability to any party for any loss, damage, or disruption caused by errors or omissions, whether such errors or omissions result from negligence, accident, or any other cause.

Dedications

I dedicate this book to all the struggling entrepreneurs, who despite their best efforts find themselves struggling in business.

I also dedicate this book to my gorgeous wife Gayle, without you it probably would never have been published. Thanks for putting up with me, it really is appreciated. Love George

Table of Contents

Introduction *5*
Mindset *6*
Initial Set Up *13*
How to get more leads *22*
Convert and retain more clients *59*
Make bigger margins *64*
Get clients to buy more often *67*
Summary *68*

Introduction

For a business to survive, it needs sales. Without leads, there can be no sales, and as such there can be no business.

Equipping yourself as a business owner with the ability to generate leads and market your business is essential if your business is going to grow and thrive.

The ideas, techniques and strategies within this book will benefit you in the following ways:

- You'll understand where you want to be
- You'll have a multitude of ways to generate new leads
- You'll have a better more profitable business
- You'll no longer have to rely on one method of generating leads
- You'll pull ahead of your competitors
- You'll be less stressed as you'll know exactly where your business is going

Incorporate these tips into your business and watch your business take off over the next 60 days. When you are ready to come back for more.

Mindset

Work every day on your business.

This is the one area that so many business owners don't seem to grasp, no matter how small your enterprise you must be working on your business every day. Small business owners may have to work in and on the business until they grow to a sufficient size that allows them to hire someone to do what they were doing in the business to enable them to work on the business. You must become the puppeteer in your business and not the puppet.

Let your personality shine in your business

Now more than at any point in history is it more important to let your personality shine through in your business. Clients buy from people, and your clients are no different. One of the things that sets your business apart from all of your competitors is you, make the most of this difference.

I once knew a very successful business owner that this definition was written for, he worked in the supplies side within the civil engineering industry, his business was defined entirely by his very gregarious and humorous personality, he was a fabulous businessman who established his company in his fifties and became exceptionally successful.

Ensure that your business reflects you and you will never have any competition as there is only one of you.

Be a master of your craft

In any endeavour, if you are going to be the real success you deserve, you need to have mastered your craft. Mastery isn't being just good or good enough it is being great and knowing it. Masters of their craft don't stop learning and improving even after they have mastered their craft. Always strive to improve and innovate in your chosen field.

Often, due to modesty, we shy away from saying that we are masters of our craft. Some through overconfidence proclaim it far too soon, however, in my opinion, you will know deep within you, the point at which you have mastered your craft. It has been said that to become a master at anything you need to undertake the activity for around 10,000 hours. I don't know if that is necessary for every individual as we all learn differently and all have different natural aptitudes, but it is a fair measure.

Continually update your education

As I mentioned above in mastering your craft, it is not a one-time event. Industry develops and what you once learned may become obsolete due to new techniques, technology or products which change the way things are done forever in your industry.

With that in mind as a master of your chosen field not only are you potentially responsible for innovating within your field it is your responsibility to keep up to date with the changes in your field to ensure that you remain a master. I remember reading that if you do not update your skills, in 10 years you will be obsolete. None of us should ever strive to be obsolete, continually updating your skills will ensure you don't, and it is a lot of fun in the process.

Be passionate about what you offer

If you wish to make the job of marketing your product or service easier then having a passion for your product is one of the quickest and simplest ways to do this. It is possible to sell things that you are not passionate about, countless salespeople around the world do this every day. However, if you wish to have an enriched and fulfilling career selling your product or service, then you need to be passionate about it. How do you get passionate about it, well you focus on all the features and benefits that your product and service deliver?

A prime example of this is Nike, they sell sports shoes but nowhere in their marketing will you find them being passionate about the shoes, even although they are, which is how they make fabulous sports shoes. They focus on marketing on the result of being a top sportsperson, getting the result you want whether that is on the running track or the tennis court. They are passionate about helping top athletes reach their goals of winning.

Eliminate or delegate non-business growth activities

As the business owner, your role is to grow the business by working on it. Review the activities that you undertake within the business; any non-business growth activities should be eliminated or delegated at the earliest possible opportunity as these activities as important as they are, will stifle your business growth.

Find a mentor

One of the greatest activities you can ever undertake for lead generation is identifying and convincing a successful business person to mentor you, why? They have already walked the path you are on and can recommend specific actions and activities that will grow your business. It will also embody greater confidence in you when your prospects find out that your mentor is already highly rated by them and this benefit will accrue to you.

Be the gatekeeper

Wherever possible become the go-to person that when a potential client is looking for someone they come to you for advice as to where they may buy the product or service they are looking for. Being knowledgeable in this areas sets you apart from the competition and gives your prospects an added advantage to purchasing from you when they need your product or service.

Invest in your knowledge / personal development

The game of business is played mainly between the ears of the business owner. As the business owner not only do you need to be continually updating your knowledge and skills you also should be working on your personal development. One of the main reasons businesses are not as successful as they could be is that the owner has fear about one thing for another. Working on your personal development can eliminate these fears and drive your business forward in ways that you would not believe possible. Invest in yourself continually you will not believe the difference it makes in your business and your life.

Surround yourself with people who are committed to your development

Surround yourself with people who are committed to your success, anyone who is not committed to your success will be a toxic influence on you regardless of how strong a character you happen to be. It is difficult as you grow and your business grows for some of those around us to be committed to our success because it challenges their inertia, that is their issue and as such if they cannot support you then they have no right to be in your life.

Let your unique self shine through

As I said earlier there is only one of you on the planet and as such use that uniqueness in your business to be unique. I have already discussed above letting your personality shine through in business. There will be a multitude of ways that you are unique, and you should make the best of these unique attributes in every aspect of your business.

Make your business serve you

Most business owners, unfortunately, become slaves to their business and not the other way about. You must quickly make your business serve you, and it must bring you increased revenue for reduced time spent on it. This is how you must drive every aspect of your business forward. Break the chains of your business and make sure it sets you free to live the life of your design.

Initial Set Up

Begin with the end in mind

Although not a direct marketing or lead generation activity, Setting out the direction of your business is required to ensure that all of your lead generation activities are geared towards going in that direction. Also, ensuring that you know exactly where you are going is key, ensuring that your staff training is carried out most efficiently and effectively.

I want you to decide what your business will look like in five or ten years time or at the point in which you wish to exit your business.

- How large will your business be?
- Will it be local, national or international?
- How many premises will it have?
- Where will they be?
- How many staff will you have?
- Who will it be selling to?
- What will they be saying about your product or service?
- What product or services will you be selling?
- How much will you be selling?

- What will your turnover be?
- How much profit will you be making?
- How will you exit the business?

Define your niche

Defining your niche is one of the most critical parts of your lead generation process. It allows you to laser focus your marketing activity in a narrow market and will enable you to be more effective and profitable. There is a saying if you chase two rabbits you will catch neither and this is the same in marketing.

Firstly, you will know whether you sell to consumers, business to business or a combination of both. This is the first step in defining your niche. Next step is to decide who precisely it is you wish to do business with and also reviewing what your existing clients have in common.

What are your skills and experience? Have you, for instance, worked all your life serving the small business market? Or in small retail stores? Does this afford you a unique perspective in delivering for those markets? Of course, it does.

Define your target client

One of my marketing mentors said to me once if you could establish that your ideal client was a 6ft 2 male with white hair, then you could go out in the street and find them. Your definition should try to get as laser focused as that and in doing so will make every lead generation activity you undertake more efficient.

In defining your target client, you can begin to see the world from their perspective, what are their needs and wants and how can you ensure that your product or service meets these wants. Remember that clients always buy what they want, not what they need. It is ideal that your product or service meets both their needs and wants.

Create a position for your business

This subject is so vast it could fill an entire book, and there have been books written on the subject. Whether you have defined the position of your business or not, your business already has a position in the market place. How is this possible? Well, it is straightforward your business is defined with the perception of your clients/prospects in relation to other businesses. Think about your buying behaviour, you will have a myriad of options to purchase a particular product or service, you decide on whom to buy from for a variety of reasons, but one of them will be how good you perceive the business to be in relation to their competitors.

Unless you define your position, you will always be at the mercy of your clients' perception. I remember reading that self coronation is an absolute necessity in today's marketplace. I would agree to a point, provided you are as good as you say you are.

In defining your position review how good your business is in relation to others in the marketplace. Are you the best? If you are, do your clients and prospects know that you are? If not then you need to educate and inform your clients and prospects about how, and why you are the number one in your field. If you are not number one then where does your business fit in the marketplace. Remember even if you are not number one, not all is lost. A very famous car hire company positioned themselves as second place in the market and then used the "we try harder" strap-line in all their marketing an exceptionally effective way to acknowledge where you sit in the market place but to also offer your clients/prospects a reason why to buy from you.

Why should I buy from you

Every business that currently exists is unique. Why because every person is unique and they bring some level of differentiation to their marketplace whether they realise this or not. Your role as the business owner is to understand your differentiation and to educate and inform your prospects why they should buy from you rather than one of your competitors. In doing this, you need to be able to answer all of your prospects potential objections and to consider the so what's that they might say when you are explaining your uniqueness to them. So if you were saying that your client should buy from you because you were the first business to deliver your product in the world, a client might say so what to that I can get similar elsewhere. But if being the first meant that your product or service was so innovative that none of your competitors would ever match it due not only to your longevity but also your constant and never-ending innovation and that you can do so within a price point that none of your competitors can match, this is a much better explanation although only an example. Take the time to answer this question and imbue everything in your marketing with the answer to it.

Calculate the lifetime value of your client

In the section on creating an irresistible offer, I mention the calculation of the lifetime value of a client. This is important as it allows you to realise the real value of a new client, and also allows you to adjust your marketing spend to obtain that client. Let's assume for a minute that the lifetime value of your client is £10,000 would you still be content in spending only £10 to acquire this client. I am betting that you wouldn't.

To calculate your lifetime value, you need the following three figures.
- Gross profit per sale (The sale value minus only the direct cost of fulfilment)
- Number of times they buy from you annually (This can be averaged out over a number of years as required)
- The number of years that they buy from you

Once you have these three figures you can calculate the lifetime value so say your figures are as follows: £200 profit per sale three purchases per annum for five years your lifetime value would be £3,000. Knowing this allows you to determine that you can afford to spend £1,000 on obtaining the first sale and still make a £2,000 profit overall.

Decide how much of that lifetime value to invest in your marketing

Using your lifetime value above determine how much of this you will invest in acquiring a client for the first time as you can see from the example above knowing this value allowed you far greater flexibility in determining your marketing spend.

Study and master copywriting

The single biggest misunderstanding I see in business owners is that they think they are in the business of whatever their undertaking is. Business owners are in the business of marketing their undertaking. To do this effectively, you must study and master copywriting. Why your success or otherwise will be determined by how well you can explain to your clients the benefits and advantages of your product or service. You must be able to see the product or service from their perspective, what's in it for them, how will it make their life better or easier, how will it save them time or money. To do that effectively then you need to be a master copywriter.

I always advise business owners that they should undertake their own copywriting. I do this not because, no matter how good the copywriter is they will never have the passion that you have for your product or service. When you merge that passion with skilled copywriting then you have a killer combination and one that you will make your business very profitable.

Write conversationally

The key to engaging with your clients through your writing is to write conversationally when a prospect reads your sales letters, emails, brochures or web pages; it should be like you were sitting opposite them talking to them. Taking them through the features and benefits, most importantly the benefits of your offer and what is in it for them. Writing grammatically correct sales letters will quickly bore your prospects, and once that happens they will stop reading, and you've lost them as a client.

Start and maintain a swipe file of good ads, brochures

One of the things that great copywriters and direct marketers do is they create a swipe file of good ads, brochures, sales letters etc. Why do they do this? Well by studying great copywriting you improve your writing, and also it stimulates ideas for offers. You might see something in a completely unrelated field that you can adjust for your product or service and make an offer that without exposure to that copy you may never have thought of. One key element here is that you never copy someone else's writing, use this swipe file as inspiration, it will stimulate ideas, and by writing your copy, you will always produce better quality offers for your product or service.

Actively build your network

Building your network is a serious pursuit, and you should do this with energy and importance. Look for ways to build your network and identify whom you want to be in your network and actively go out of your way to network with these people.

How to get more leads

Create an irresistible offer

Obtaining clients is the single most difficult activity that you will undertake in business, it is the key to actually being in business. If you have no clients, you have no business. To convince a prospect to buy from you the first time, you must make them an offer they can't refuse. This offer must remove any potential barrier they might have for not buying your product or service. Knowing your lifetime value of your clients will be key to creating this offer. Craft your irresistible offer carefully based on where your business is currently, some businesses will be able to afford to lose on the initial acquisition of the client as their lifetime value is so great that the business can afford to make a loss on this first acquisition. Never gamble in this area. Make your offer irresistible but don't risk the business. There are many ways to ensure that you can make your offer irresistible, even if your business is not cash rich.

Reverse the risk of the sale

In any purchasing situation, one half of a purchase bears all the risk. If you want to ensure the maximum number of conversions you must reverse the risk of the purchase, so you might do it like this. Try this product at home for 30 days and if you are not satisfied with it, return it to me, and I will refund all of your purchase price no questions asked.

I am sure that you can see how powerful that statement is and how convincing it would be to a prospect. If you offer services or consultancy, you may need to tailor the risk reversal to make it conditional that the client, has carried out what you have recommended or advised. It might go something like this. If after using this service you remain dissatisfied in any way I will refund 100% of the cost of the service, provided you can provide me with detailed evidence that you have undertaken all of the activities I have recommended you take.

Explain the features and benefits of your product or service

It is often asked if a sales letter, brochure or web page can be too long. The answer to this is it can never be too long only too boring. A two-page sales letter will outsell a one-page letter; a four-page will outsell a two page and so on. The key to any sales letter is to explain in detail the features and benefits of your offer to your client. You would never say to your top sales person I want you to go out to a sales meeting, and you can only present for 5 minutes or say 1,000 words that would be insane. You must explain all of the features and benefits of your product or service in sufficient detail so that you are informing and educating your prospect on what is in it for them as that is the only thing they care about.

Give your reasons why

As well as explaining in detail the features and benefits of your product or service, you must also explain to them the reasons why you can offer this product or service to them. If you had a stock room full of your product and you had to get rid of it before the end of the season, you would explain to your prospect that you must make room in your stockroom for your new season stock and that is why you are having a 75% off sale. If you merely offered a 75% reduction, your client may think that it is inferior quality stock and as such not buy it. Do you see the powerful nature of explaining the reasons why to your clients?

Create a prospects list

You have now been undertaking your lead generation activities, and you now have prospects putting up their hand identifying that they are interested in your product or service. An important part of managing this process is to create a detailed prospect list with as much detail about the client as possible that will stack the odds of conversion in your favour.

Keep a list of lapsed buyers

You've sold to your client the first time, and over a period of time, they stop purchasing from you. Keep a list of these lapsed buyers and offer them opportunities to buy from you again at preferential rates, why? Well, it is significantly more expensive to get a new client as it is to sell to an existing client on that basis if you can reactivate this lapsed buyer then you are reaching them at virtually no cost to the business beyond the hard cost of whatever incentive you give them to buy again from you.

Also, if there is a particular reason why they stopped purchasing from you, then this information is key to improving your product or service and increasing the quality of your offer. It is said that calm seas never made a good sailor and also in business the clients who are unhappy with your product will offer you greater opportunity to improve and give additional service to your clients. Never ignore a lapsed client and ensure where possible that if they were unhappy with your product or service that you take on board their views and improve your product or service accordingly.

Publish your presentations on slide-share

You are an expert in your field; you regularly present to groups. Take these presentations and publish them on slide-share sites. This increases your standing within your industry as your expertise is out there and will increase your standing within your prospects mind. Incidentally, if you are not presenting on your subject regularly, then you should be. Take every opportunity to present in your field or demonstrate your expertise in other ways if presentations are not suitable in your field.

Write a book

It has been said that everyone has at least one book in them. Writing a book will increase your positioning as an expert in your field and providing you have actually been in your field or studied it extensively then you are an expert and deserve to be recognised as one.

Educate your clients impartially

Your role as the business owner is to educate and inform your clients impartially as to the benefits of your product or service. Your role is not to sell to them at any cost as that is counterproductive in the long run. If after eduction your product or service is not right for your prospect then you must tell them and if possible recommend an alternative solution which is a good fit for them. Not only does this ensure that the prospect gets the service or product they want they will also tell everyone that you are a business to be trusted to give impartial advice and won't just sell to you no matter what.

Create your website

In this digital age, it amazes me that there are still significant numbers of business that do not have a website. If you do not have a website then you must get one even if it isn't going to be the mainstay of your business activity, it is essential to have one.

Create landing pages

Never send a prospect directly to your corporate website. To effectively grow your business, you must create landing pages where all new prospects are directed. This landing page must only allow your prospect to do two things, either give you their name and email address or leave your page. You must incentivise your prospect to give you their name and email address by giving them something of value in exchange for their details. This is normally a free report or video recording which is of value to them. Once they give you their details on your opt-in form you can then utilising the power of autoresponders, send them information which will move them along in your marketing funnel until they make a purchase.

Constantly drive traffic to your landing page

You've created a lead page giving your project valuable information in return for their name and email address. Now that the lead page is live, constantly drive traffic to the page. You can utilise many of the techniques above to drive traffic to your lead page and have your prospect join your funnel.

Create an opt-in form on your website

As well as your landing page have an opt-in form on your website. This allows you to capture prospects who for whatever reason have found your main website to opt-in to obtain your free report and to allow you to market to them.

Create an online store

Imagine waking in the morning and having received money overnight while you slept. Not a bad way of earning is it. Creating an online store allows your shop to be online and operational 24 hours a day across the globe. Even traditional bricks and mortar businesses can benefit from an online store as our prospects channel shift to buying products and services online as opposed to in stores or in person.

Blog

One of the best things you can do for your web presence and positioning is to create a blog and to post informative and interesting content to your blog regularly. It is very important that when creating your blog that you create and maintain a schedule of regular writing whether that is once a day, three time a week, or once a week. Why? Your blog readers want to follow what you are saying, and if you do not commit to regular publication, they are busy people and will find other things to do with their time.

Highlight new content on your blog

Whatever platform or content management system you use to manage your blog make sure that you highlight what is new on your blog so that a reader can easily identify your new content from the stuff they have already consumed. It saves them time when they reach your blog and they will thank you for it by continued support for your blog.

Keyword research

Researching keywords is a must for your product or service. It is much better to identify a need and fill it that to create a product or service and then try to find a need for it. Identifying the keywords that you will use in your search engine optimisation, within your ads on your website and in articles and literature that you publish online will improve the number of prospects who will find you as a result of organic searches on the internet. There are a number of free and paid for keyword research tools available depending on your needs.

Search Engine Optimisation

SEO or search engine optimisation is often considered a dark art, and in some cases, it has been. The search engines are cracking down on unscrupulous use of SEO and if you are employing these on your website then shame on you. Good search engine optimisation will improve your reach and the number of visitors reaching your site through organic searches. SEO can be very expensive, but everything you do on your site and all of the literature that you produce and publish on the internet must be search engine optimised.

Link to other related websites

Linking to other related websites is still a very effective way of increasing your page rank. Although an effective strategy, you need to be careful that the links you have with your site are related to your product or service area or you may find that the links do not improve your page-rank and have the reverse effect.

Create an elevator speech

A very simple yet effective way of succinctly capturing the benefits of what you do is to create an elevator speech. An elevator speech must capture what is in it for your client in the time it would take to ride up in an elevator. It could be something like the following:

Frustrated with having poor looking hair that is out of condition and with grey roots, my salon takes the time to get to know exactly what your hair needs are to ensure that you leave our salon happy and with the most gorgeous cut and vibrant colour you have ever experienced.

Build credibility by writing for publications

As entrepreneurs, we are constantly building and maintaining our credibility in the eyes of our prospects and existing clients. A very good way to build credibility is to write for publications that our prospects read. Getting opportunities to write for these publications is sometimes as easy as simply pitching to the right person within the publication. Provided you have interesting and informative articles that fit with the publications requirements, including your articles helps the publisher in ensuring that they have good quality content for their readers.

Write reports and white papers

Whatever industry you are in you should commit to writing reports or white papers in your niche. These reports should be written in an informative and impartial manner and should act to educate and inform your prospects. These reports should not be sales orientated but can include links to offers you currently have available. Be careful however if your reports / white papers are seen as blatant sales pitches then it will turn your prospect off.

Write articles and publish them

Similar to writing reports and white papers writing and publishing articles on your area of specialism, will position you as the go-to expert in your field. Also writing articles will drive traffic to your website and increase your search engine rankings with the links back to your website.

Network

It is often said that the sum of your network can measure your net worth, while I do not necessarily agree with this, effective networking in any business is essential. It is essential for a number of reasons but getting a referral from a network partner is a very effective way to gain new clients and to identify good quality prospects.

When at networking events be active in making the new contacts you want to make

One of the biggest errors I see and unfortunately have committed myself at networking events is to be less than active in making the connections that you want to make at networking events. Before any networking event or event which there is an opportunity to network you should set out what your end goal is for the event. Whom do you want to network with, how will you follow up these contacts. If someone is very popular how will you get the opportunity to meet with them or to exchange your information with them.

Referrals

As I have discussed above in network referrals are a very powerful strategy for growing your business. To get the most referrals though you must incentivise the referer to give the referral if you are going to be as successful as you would like to be with this strategy. One of the biggest mistakes I see with referral rewards is to give the referer a gift of something which is not related to your service in any way. A hair salon for instance, if one of your existing clients refers one of their friends who is currently a client don't give them a bottle of champagne or shopping vouchers unless those vouchers are redeemable only against purchases within your salon.

Business cards

Business cards can be a very effective way of obtaining new business provided they are used correctly. Your business card should give your name, but it must be specific about the benefits and advantages of your product or service. I would also recommend that you do not print your telephone number on the card but take the time to handwrite and give it to your prospect I find this adds a very personal touch.

Host event or workshop

Hosting events or workshops can be a very effective way of gaining new business. An effective way that I have seen this done is to host a number of free events with these events will educate and inform your prospects and with the purpose of filling a paid for event at some time in the future. This gives you the opportunity to showcase your skills and to educate and inform your prospects.

Tell everyone what you do

This may seem obvious, but it amazes me the number of business owners who don't tell their friends and people they come into contact with actually know what it is they do. Tell everyone what you do, tell them what the benefits of your product or service is and ask if there is anyone that they know who might be interested in your product or service. You don't want to bore them with your constant self-promotion, but I assume that your product or service has many benefits so if you don't get the information out there to the people who want your service you are doing them a disservice.

Create strategic alliances / joint ventures

One of the greatest ways to grow your business is through the creation of strategic alliances / joint ventures with complementary but non-competing businesses. Review your ideal client profile, identify who already has these existing clients who are not in direct competition with you and approach them to do a joint venture. A few things to keep in mind when doing this is that the partner must be the one who approaches their clients and makes the recommendation that they use your service, the partner must have an active client list who they are in regular contact with and it must be a buyers list not a prospects list and finally you need to give the partner a substantial cut of the profit to ensure it is worth their while and that they are compelled to want to take part.

Speaking your way to more clients

Speaking is a wonderful way to increase your positioning in your marketplace and is a very powerful way of gaining new business. I know of many speakers who even when speaking for free at conferences and seminars earn a substantial amount of money from product or service sales either at the end of the speech or during the breaks in the seminar or conference.

Capture your content by recording your speech

Whenever or wherever you speak ensure that you can record the speech both video and audio. I know of a very successful internet marketer who had a seminar during the start-up phase of his business. He managed only to convince a small number of attendees; however, he recorded the event and sold the video of the event and made a huge profit. Utilising and repurposing the recordings allows you to create other products and lead generation reports, video excerpts, audio recordings, publications such as books or reports from something you are already doing anyway. One of my mentors once said to me that whenever you speak make sure that you record it and it is great advice.

Ensure everyone dresses professionally

Depending on your industry there will be a standard of professional dress that is expected of you. Sales staff almost always are expected to be dressed in a suit mostly wearing ties. So whatever industry you are in ensure that you and your staff always dress professionally. I often see in the beauty industry staff members who look like they have just been dragged through a hedge backwards. This is not the image that you want your business or staff to portray.

Join your professional association

Join the professional body that represents your industry. Become actively involved with the professional body and if possible volunteer to assist at their events etc. Prospects are always searching for ways to trust you and you being a member of the professional organisation representing your industry is one of the things they look for.

Create an exciting brochure

Brochures like sale letters should be exciting, not dull and boring. I have mentioned earlier your letters and brochures can never be too long only too boring. Ensure that you invest in the production of your brochure and take time to explain the benefits and advantages to the client of purchasing from you through your brochure.

Record your best sales person and use it as a script for training all your other staff

Identify the most successful salesperson you have and record their sales pitch, use that sales pitch too train your other sales staff and make sure that they follow that script when pitching to prospects.

Teleconferences

A favourite of mine is the teleconference, now being overshadowed a bit by webinars teleconferences have the benefit that you only need access to a phone and that you can pretty much conduct them from anywhere on the planet. During teleconferences, you have the opportunity to explain your product or service in detail to your prospect and to interact with them and answer any questions that they may have. Ensure that you also record your teleconferences.

Accept credit cards and electronic payments

Make it easy for your clients to purchase from you by ensuring you can take credit card and electronic payment for your product or services. Every activity that you perform should make it easy for your prospect to purchase from you. There are numerous electronic payment platforms these days, so there is no excuse for not having them in your business.

Create email signature

How many emails do you write a day, week or a month? I'm guessing that there will be a substantial amount of them if you are anything like me. Well combining a link to your free report or lead page will give an opportunity for anyone receiving your email to see the benefit of your offer and to click through on the link and join your prospect sales funnel.

Use surveys

What better way to create a perfect product or service is there than asking your clients and prospects what it is they want, how they want to receive it and how much they might be willing to pay for it. Conducting surveys has probably never been easier than now in the internet age, use them to design perfect offerings and you will overcome much of the resistance from your prospects because you have tailored your offering to exactly what they are looking for.

Sponsor an event

One of the best ways to obtain £1,000's of free publicity is by the sponsoring of an event. It may be that your business is entirely local and it would then make sense to sponsor a local event. If it is more national, it may be a series of events across the country. This is a win-win activity as an event gets needed sponsorship and as part of your participation, you get welcome exposure for your business.

Prominently support a charity

I am always in favour of businesses supporting charitable causes and not just for the exposure that it may gain your business. I think it is incumbent on all successful businesses to give back to the communities that support us and as such, it is like sponsoring events a win-win activity.

Obtain testimonials

One of the most powerful marketing strategies that you can employ within your business is the testimonial. Make whatever claims you want about your business they will remain just that, a claim. Have a satisfied client give you a testimony, and that becomes a fact. One of the best exponents of this strategy is Jay Abraham. He is a marketing genius and has thousands of testimonials which are extremely powerful in terms of his position as a marketing genius.

Do joint seminars / speak at others seminars

I have already described how powerful a strategy it is to speak and to hold your events and seminars, take every opportunity to speak at other businesses events and do joint seminars and events with similar but non-competing businesses. It is highly likely that their clients will also be interested in your offer, so it makes sense to take these opportunities to have a captive audience to educate on the benefits of your product or services.

Ask clients what they want

Most if not all of your competitors are only concerned with selling their product to their prospects, few if any will ever ask their clients/prospects what they want. Do not make this mistake in your business frequently ask your clients what they want.

Ask them how they want your product/service delivered

As well as asking them what they want also ask them how they want your product or service delivered. I don't know of any smarter strategy than asking your client what they want and how they want not delivered then giving it to them exactly as they have asked for it.

Become a local radio / TV personality

Becoming a local radio or tv personality is a very good way to attract new leads and business. You need to have something newsworthy to say or to be available to comment on current affairs concerning your area of expertise. Make a point of contacting your local radio and tv stations with a view to being a guest on their shows. You'll be surprised at how often you'll get asked to be on their shows.

Celebrity endorsement

Few strategies can be more powerful than a celebrity endorsement. If you don't believe me research, George Foreman grills what an outstanding endorsement of a celebrity endorsement. There are countless celebrities, local, national and international, who know the power of endorsement and are actively seeking out brands to endorse.

Teach a class at your local college/university

It has often been said that if you truly want to learn something, teach it. Your skills will improve measurably as you deepen your knowledge of things that you took for granted in your field, but realise is key when teaching it. Colleges and Universities are keen to broaden their appeal and make money, so a well attended class taught by you will fit well within their overall business plan.

Network with the main players in your industry/service

Take every opportunity to network with the main players in your industry, you will learn from them in ways you won't believe just by being in the same space as them and listening to what they have to say. Also networking with them you might even find yourself a key mentor who will assist in your growth.

Scientific advertising

The best book on advertising I ever read is Scientific Advertising by Claude Hopkins. If you haven't read it get a copy, you will learn more about advertising in those pages than most people will ever learn in their lives. The key to all advertising that you do is to ensure that it is scientific. You ensure that all advertising you do is measurable by sales and by coding the advert, so you know where that sale came from. Your coding can be anything you like but make sure that every ad you ever undertake has a code that ensures you can measure the result of the advert. Through this and testing only one element of your advert at a time, you can quickly get to the point where your results are predictable.

Social proof

We live in the era of social media, and it has never been easier and more difficult to grab the attention of your prospects. Building your tribe of like-minded people who want your product or service is key to this social proof, and you can do this in a number of ways. Building your social proof through your books, your website, facebook page, twitter account are all effective ways to market your business and build your social proof.

Market online

With billions of people online it would be insane to avoid marketing your business online. There are a myriad of different ways to market online and far too many for me to define in this short space. Ensure that like advertising all of your marketing is scientific and that you identify and solve your prospects problems.

Market offline

With the increase in the internet many businesses are only utilising online marketing opportunities, and although these can be extremely attractive, there is still a place for good offline marketing and your marketing strategy should contain a mix of offline and online marketing. Often because of the reduction in offline marketing, you can get a huge boost by incorporating a few offline marketing strategies into your marketing mix. Ensure that your business takes the opportunity to market offline as well as online. Measure the results of each and adjust accordingly.

Utilise public relations

Advertising is very expensive, the least expensive way to get your business into a print or online magazine or publication is through effective public relations. Create a public relations strategy for your business, create offers based on specific dates so on 5 May, you can create a Cinco De Mayo offer and by utilising public relations obtain thousands of pounds of free advertising. As always with public relations be newsworthy, and you won't go far wrong.

Use direct mail

With the advent of the internet, many thought it would spell the end of direct mail. In my experience, it is far from the truth, and a good direct mail piece to a good responsive buyer list can deliver huge benefits to your overall marketing strategy. I have seen a two step approach where a direct mail piece directs you to a lead page with a very attractive offer sometimes with a good video piece delivering real quality to your prospect. Direct mail is a very effective way of driving sales and should be incorporated into your overall marketing mix.

Ask everyone if they know anyone who might need your service

You interact on a daily basis with many people either in person, through your social media accounts, email or website and while doing this, you should make a point of asking people if they know anyone who might want your product or service.

Take part in discussion forums

Discussion forums are great places to interact with your prospects. Forums are very well monitored, and if you are blatantly sales orientated, you will find that you are removed from the forum. However, provided you are providing the members of the forum with useful information, that solves their problems, and your response has a link to your lead page you can increase highly targeted traffic to your lead page by this activity.

Solve others problems in forums

The whole point of engaging with your audience in forums is to solve their problems. Prospects, as I have mentioned before, do not care about you, their reason for being on the forum is usually because they have a problem and they are looking for a solution to that problem. Solve their problems and they will be very receptive to your message and your marketing.

Automate your marketing systems

Automation is one of the key benefits of the internet, no longer do we need to be chained too our desk constantly replying to emails from prospects and clients. Through the process of automation, we can now operate our business from anywhere in the world 24 hours per day. Utilise automation systems in your marketing and you will reap huge rewards.

Review and publish an impartial report on your industry or field

As I have mentioned numerous times in this book, be impartial. Review and publish an impartial report on your industry or field. Become that true authority in your area of business, explain what works and what could be improved in an impartial way for all of your competitors and your service. This should be an informative writing piece not in anyway sales driven.

Rent lists

Made famous in the direct mail market renting lists can be a very effective tool in increasing your business. The list broker will be able to explain to you the lists they have available, how responsive they are, and the cost to rent the list. These lists must always be buyer lists as any other type of list will not bring you the responsiveness you desire.

Create a product/service video

It has never been easier to produce quality video than now. Almost every smartphone has a high definition camera capable of producing a good quality video, and with sites like Youtube, it's never been easier to have your video content on the internet. Utilising this very powerful technology you can create lead capture video content. Think of the problems that your clients have and that your product or service is the solution for and create video content that solves their problems.

Create a detailed marketing plan

Creating a detailed marketing plan is key to marketing your business. Your plan must cover in detail every marketing activity that you will undertake over the course of the time frame of the plan.

As a minimum, your marketing plan must cover who your target clients are and if you have done the work above you will already know this. How you are going to reach these target clients and how you will retain them.

There are many templates for marketing plans; however, I have included a number of key headings below that will allow you to create a detailed marketing plan of your own:

- Summary of your plan

  This should be a summary of the entire plan and is usually written last.

- Target Clients

  Utilising the work you have done above defining your target client in detail

- Why they should buy from you

  Often referred to as your unique selling point or proposition, this should be worked on in sufficient detail not only to define your unique selling point but also so you can answer the so what questions that your client may respond with when reviewing your USP.

- Your positioning

  Where you are positioned in the marketplace. This can be a wide or narrow definition. If you only work locally you could define your business as the best in the local area even if you weren't the best in the entire country.

- Your irresistible offers

  This is one of your keys for generating new business, removing the barrier to buy from you the first time. Take time to craft your offer taking account of the lifetime value of your client and ensuring that you invest enough of that lifetime profit to remove the risk for them of buying from you the first time.

- Your marketing materials

  This should include your brochures and literature used in marketing your business.

- How you will promote your business

  This should consider and detail how you are going to market to your target audience, will this be through events, trade shows, writing, speaking, advertising whatever ways you decide to market your business they need to be included here.

- How you will market online

It is essential to market online now, although I see multiple businesses who have no or very poor online presence, this leaves money on the table and is very inefficient. This section of your plan will specify and detail how you will research and define the keywords you use in your website and your paid for advertising, how you will optimise your website, paid adverts and social media posts to table the highest organic ranking through search engine optimisation and how you will use your social media presence to drive prospects to your landing pages and offers.

- How you will get your prospects to buy

    How will you get your prospects to buy from you the first time? Crafting your irresistible offer and utilising your lifetime value of a client is key in this area. There after you need to over deliver on your promise in your offer and nurture your clients to buy from you continually.

- What strategic alliances you will form

    One of the most powerful marketing strategies you can undertake is creating strategic alliances with complimentary non competing businesses. Simply find non competing complimentary businesses who already have your target clients, approach those businesses and provided they have an up to date comprehensive list of active buyers, create a joint venture with them that will have them recommend your product or service to their list. It is key that they recommend you to their list as their clients trust them. Ensure also that you make it worth their while, I would suggest that the minimum profit share for them should be 25% or more depending on your lifetime value. The key is to get them to agree to the joint venture. If for instance, you have a very high retention rate and a very high lifetime value you could afford to give your alliance partner the entire profit from the initial offer to obtain the client.

- What your strategy is for referrals

    Like strategic alliances referrals are an exceptionally effective way to obtain your, clients. Every claim you make in your marketing materials is just that to a prospect a claim. Every recommendation from a referral partner is a fact they are recommending you because the know your product or service and have bought and trust you to deliver what you say you will to your clients. So define how you will obtain referrals and what you will give your referer in return for the referral.

- How you will increase the frequency and amount your clients buy from you

    You have a client who is buying from you three times per year, how are you going to increase the number of times that they buy from you? You could consider offering them an overall discount on the purchase price of your product or service on the basis that they purchase your product or service a set number of times in the year. So, for example, you have an £80 product, and your profit margin is £20 per sale. Currently, your existing client is purchasing three times per year so annually you are generating a £60 profit from this client. If you lowered your price to £75 per sale but persuaded your client to buy on a minimum of 5 times per year your profit would increase to £75 per annum an increase of 25% in total profit for the year by offering a 6.25% price reduction.

    You could alternatively offer additional bonuses or additional services at preferential rates to your client to increase the frequency of purchase and hence increase your overall profit.

- How you will retain clients

Client retention is key to your long term longevity as a business, how do you ensure that your clients remain with you long term? You over deliver on your promise to that client, you always advise them impartially and ensure that you become their trusted advisor.

- What your financial projections are

  The last part of your plan is the financial projections, utilising all of the above plan how will that increase your profit margins throughout the course of the plan. This is important as it will allow you to measure on a month by month basis what result you are getting against the projections you have made within your plan. If things are not going as well as you have predicted you can review how each element of the plan is performing and adjust as necessary. Without these, projections you will flounder around not knowing if your plan is working or optimised as well as it could be.

Create a detailed marketing calendar from your marketing plan

Taking your plan above create a marketing calendar for every marketing element within your plan. Commit to ensuring that each element is undertaken on that day, no excuses. The majority of businesses I have had experience of, do not understand this element at all. Choosing to wait until they are short of clients before undertaking usually ineffective marketing that creates small peaks in an otherwise trough like business profile.

Commit to yourself and your plan by creating a detailed marketing calendar and work that calendar everyday. It is simply the most effective tool you will employ. Imagine this if you added one new lead generation activity to your calendar every day for 30 days at the end of the 30 days you would have an additional 30 lead generating activities. The discipline of this will drive your business forward exponentially.

Implement the marketing plan and measure results

As mentioned above creating the marketing plan and the calendar will achieve nothing beyond mental stimulation for you unless you implement. When you implement each of your strategies, you will start to see results, particularly because you will encode each activity so that you know the exact result of every activity.

Simply put businesses that measure their results improve. Why? Because they can identify what is working best and from that tailor their activities to ensure that they are doing more of the most successful activities.

Adjust the marketing plan accordingly

You have created your plan, you've created the calendar you have implemented, and you have tracked and measured results. Brilliant, you are ahead of most businesses in your sector; however, it doesn't finish there. You need to adjust your plan accordingly. What activities are working best and at the lowest cost, do more of these and curtail or stop those less effective activities. Every activity you undertake is an investment compare rate of return for each and only take forward the most profitable activities.

Convert and retain more clients

Reactivate lapsed buyers

Utilising your list of lapsed buyers create an irresistible offer to get them to repurchase from you. Reactivating lapsed clients can be a very profitable activity as you already have overcome their resistance to buy the first time and you already have their details thus making them almost zero cost marketing activity.

Follow up with prospects

So you have undertaken some marketing activity a prospect has raised their hand to indicate they are interested but they don't buy immediately. Follow up all your non converting leads and continue to follow-ups until they buy or they ask you to stop contacting them. Continue to explain the benefits and advantages of your product or service to your prospect and ask them to take action. You will be amazed at the number of prospects that will buy if only you follow up with them. To quote an example a very successful mail order company followed me up as a prospect over the course of 8 years, as time went by they contacted me less frequently but they continued to write to me until I eventually bought their product and I am glad they did. The product was high quality and was exactly what I was looking for when I eventually bought it. Learn from this very experienced and successful company that following up is very successful and very profitable. The more you follow up, the greater your profits will be.

Take your client journey yourself

One of the most enlightening activities that you can undertake as a business owner is to undertake your client journey yourself. Are you making it difficult for your clients to buy from you? If you are you are lowering your conversion rates needlessly. Make it easy for clients to do business with you.

Extensively train your staff in your business vision

There is no better way to convert prospects to purchase for the first time than to extensively train each member of your staff. Your staff are the face of your business, and they represent you in every dealing with your prospect. If they don't get your overall vision and understand the detail of your business and what you are trying to achieve, then they will reduce your results measurably. Why? Your prospects are dying to be educated and informed about the benefits of your product or service, one member of staff who does not do this, will lose you that prospect most likely forever. Train your staff extensively it is one of the greatest benefits and advantages in your business make sure you use it.

Incentivise your staff to perform better and make more sales

Just as your prospects and clients are only interested in what is in it for them, so too are your staff interested in what's in it for them. Incentivise your staff, so they want to perform better, and with that, they reap the rewards of their industry. Create an entrepreneurial atmosphere in your business, allow staff to share in the rewards of your increased profitability. Provided your business is profitable why shouldn't your staff be well rewarded for what they do, ensure that the reward is based directly on their performance.

Have a system which handles your existing clients

As you implement these tips, your business is going to grow and grow substantially. As your business grows make sure that the systems you have in place to manage your clients' information and data are sufficiently robust that they can cope with the additional workload that managing increases in clients and prospects entail.

There is no point in putting in significant investment in your marketing to have your database programme crash and lose all of the data.

Be organised

Having increased clients and prospects requires you to be organised to ensure that you can manage them and their expectation. I remember one of my marketing mentors telling me that if my business wasn't ready to handle a huge influx of clients not to use the techniques he had taught me until I was. Wise words.

Always give greater value

I am sure that your business gives your clients great value, however, as the business owner, your role should be to consistently seek to give your clients greater value in every product or service you deliver. Giving greater value will lead to increases in referrals and easier conversions. Always seek to innovate and give greater value in everything that you do.

Follow up every sale

One of the easiest ways that you can position your business above all others you compete against is by following up the sale. Often a first-0time purchaser can experience buyers remorse, but by following them up and answering any questions or doubts your client may have, you will reassure them and lower the instance of buyers remorse.

Ask every post-sale client how you can improve your service/product

So you have a product or service which is selling well, that's your job done is it not? No, it's not. Following every sale during your follow above take the opportunity to ask every client how you can improve your product or service. You'll be amazed at how much information and advantage this will give you over everyone you compete against.

Make it easy and pleasurable to do business with you

When you make it easy and pleasurable to do business with you, then clients are falling over themselves to purchase your product. It is difficult enough to make the first sale to a prospect, so make the process slick and simple.

Make bigger margins

Raise your prices/fees

An area that many business owners shy away from is price raises particularly during difficult times and recession. Raising your fees may very well cause some of your existing clients to leave you and go elsewhere; however, your role as the business owner is to explain that your product or service is not a commodity and that price is only one of the determining factors in choosing whether to purchase or not. I am confident that no matter what industry you are in that you aren't charging enough for the benefit that you are delivering. Recognise this and increase your fees accordingly.

Create tiers for your product

One of the most successful ways to lower the resistance to purchase from you is to create tiers for your product with the most expensive tier being the most exclusive. There is something deeply appealing to prospects when they see that you have an elite platinum tier for your product which is exclusive and they have to apply for access. That process of having to be approved for the product or service is very appealing psychologically and lowers the resistance; prospects often feel when considering purchasing. Whatever product or service you offer, you can create packages which add value to the prospect and appeal to them.

Continually source and offer your clients complementary non competing products

One of the many benefits of taking a consultative impartial advisor role with your clients is the opportunity to identify complementary products that you can source and offer to your existing clients and new clients as an incentive to purchase from you. You could use these products as bonuses or as incentives for them to buy.

Identify the clients you don't want to work with

If you are familiar with Pareto's Law, you will understand that 80% of your revenues will come from 20% of your clients. This is also true for your business problems 80% of your problems will come from 20% of your clients. No matter how much revenue a client gives you if they are true problem clients my advice is to thank them for identifying themselves as not one of your clients. You don't need to do business with problem clients it takes up your energy and takes you away from working on your business.

Never sell purely on price

No matter the product or service you have, never sell it purely on price. Even if you are in the commodity business make sure you define for your prospects the additional reasons why they should buy your product or service over and above a good price point.

Get clients to buy more often

Market more to your most responsive buyers

It may surprise you but marketing more often to your most responsive buyers will increase your revenues significantly. If a client spends a lot with you they obviously like your product or service and giving them more frequent opportunities to buy more, will excite them and will have the added benefit that your revenues and profits will increase. Like all offers that you make you need to give genuine added value as these are your best clients so treat them as such. You might want to consider creating a membership programme for your most responsive clients where they get exclusive offers that no one else gets and that they get your offers for an exclusive period before you market to the rest of your list.

Summary

You now have 107 marketing and lead generation tips that you can implement within your business. Have fun doing this and adjust your sails accordingly.

For a more in-depth study of the above visit my website https://georgewells.co.uk

George Wells, having extensively studied all things direct marketing from the legends of yesteryear to the most innovative and current marketers brings his take on marketing and lead generation. Having studied and worked professionally for over 30 years as an engineer George is well versed is fixing problems and his passion is to assist struggling business owners to finally sort out their marketing and live the glorious life they deserve.

www.ingramcontent.com/pod-product-compliance
Lightning Source LLC
Chambersburg PA
CBHW020616220526
45463CB00006B/2597